SUPER PEGASUS
ARTISTS

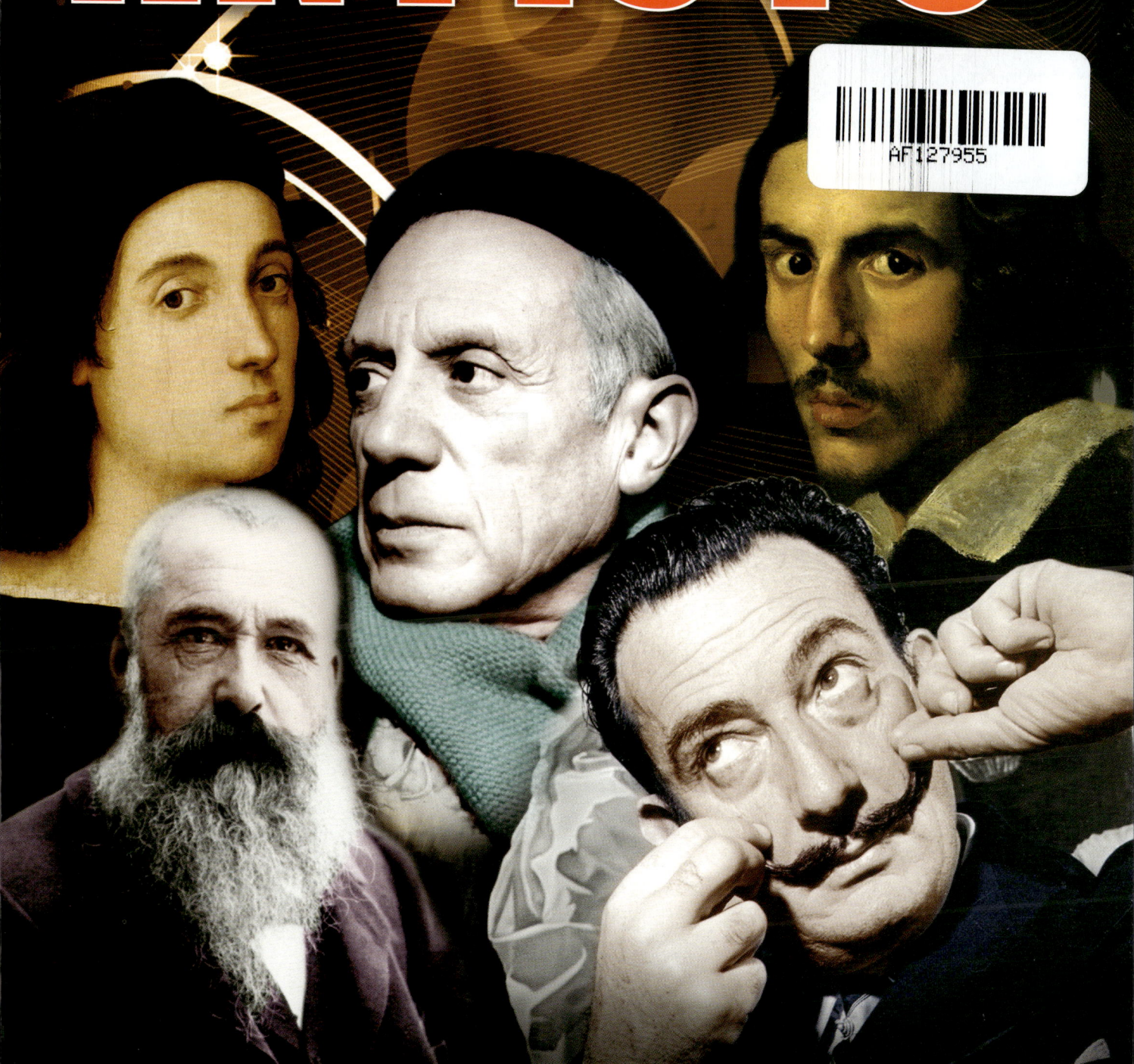

www.pegasusforkids.com

© **B. Jain Publishers (P) Ltd.** All rights reserved. No part of this book may be reproduced, stored in a retrieval system or transmitted, in any form or by any means, mechanical, photocopying, recording or otherwise, without any prior written permission of the publisher.

Published by Kuldeep Jain for B. Jain Publishers (P) Ltd., D-157, Sector 63, Noida - 201307, U.P

Printed in India

Image page nos. 3, 5, 14, 20, 21, 29, 30, 31, 36, 42, 43, 44, 48 © Copyright Getty Images India

Contents

4	Frida Kahlo
8	Giovanni Lorenzo Bernini
12	Henri Rousseau
14	M.F. Husain
16	Leonardo da Vinci
20	Michelangelo Buonarroti
24	Oscar Claude Monet
28	Pablo Picasso
32	Raphael Sanzio
36	Rembrandt Harmenszoon van Rijn
40	Salvador Dali
44	Vincent Willem van Gogh

Frida Kahlo

Self-Portrait with Thorn Necklace and Hummingbird

Artist Frida Kahlo is amongst Mexico's greatest artists. She took to painting after she was severely injured in a bus accident while she was still young. Kahlo, later in her life, was also politically active and married fellow communist artist Diego Rivera in 1929. Though her paintings were exhibited all over Mexico while she lived, she gained fame after her works were exhibited in Paris and elsewhere before her death in 1954.

Early Life

Frida was born Magdalena Carmen Frieda Kahlo y Calderón. She grew up in her family's home—later referred to as the Blue House or Casa Azul. Her father, Wilhelm, was a German photographer who had immigrated to Mexico, where he met and married her mother Matilde. Frida was the third among their four children. Around the age of six, Frida contracted polio. Though she was cured but the disease had damaged her right leg and foot. In order to help her recover, her father, to whom she was quite close, encouraged her to exercise and take up sports. She took her father's advice and started running, swimming, and boxing amongst others. Interestingly, most of these activities were meant only for boys at that time. With time, she became better but had to walk with a limp.

Studies and Injury

In school, despite her physical setbacks, Frida was known for her cheerful spirit and for her love for traditional and colourful clothes and jewellery. While still in school, she first saw famed Mexican muralist Diego Rivera, who was commissioned to do a project in her school. Frida often watched over as Rivera created a mural called *The Creation,* in the school's lecture hall.

While at school, Frida hung out with a group of political and intellectual like-minded students. She was intelligent and her group used to exchange ideas and discuss about the politics of the country. A few years later, the bus she was travelling in, collided with a streetcar. Frida received severe injuries as a steel handrail pierced her hip. She also suffered fractures in her spine, leg and pelvis. It was a long and painful recovery for 18-year-old Frida as she was put in a full-body cast. During this time, she started to paint. Her mother had a special easel made for her, so she could paint while she was in bed recovering from her injuries. Her father also lent her his oil colours. Frida finished her first self-portrait the following year. Post recovery, she joined the Young Communist League and the Mexican Communist Party, becoming more politically active. Though she had recovered but all her life she continued to experience great pain, which left her bedridden from days to months. She had had as many as 35 operations during her life as a result of the fatal accident.

Tumultuous Marriage

Frida again met Rivera in 1928. He saw her artwork and encouraged her to paint. In time, Rivera started coming to her house and gave her insights into her paintings. Frida used these insights to make improvisations in her paintings. Soon the two began a relationship. In time, the two got married. Frida's works were also influenced by Mexican culture and she shows this in her work through the use of bright colours and dramatic symbolism. Most of her works are self-

Frida with Rivera

Roots Raices

portraits, as she puts it, 'I am the subject I know best.'

Interestingly, although Frida and Rivera were married, they stayed in separate houses and studios. Signs of trouble were evident in their marriage right from the onset. Living separately was the last resort that they had. The couple divorced in 1939 but a year later, they married again. However, their second term in marriage was as troublesome as the first. Often Frida went along with Rivera wherever he was commissioned to do work. During one such trip to San Francisco, Frida showed her painting, *Frieda and Diego Rivera,* at the Sixth Annual Exhibition of the San Francisco Society of Women Artists.

Gradually, she incorporated more graphic and surrealistic elements in her works. In her painting, *Henry Ford Hospital* (1932), one of her deeply personal work, she shows her grief over her inability to bear children.

Art and Self-Portraits

Though her works had elements of surrealism but she never thought them to be so. In 1938, she had a major exhibition at a New York City gallery, selling half of the 25 paintings on display there. She also received two commissions, including one from famed magazine editor Clare Boothe Luce, as a result of the show.

In 1939, Frida went to live in Paris for some time to exhibit her work. Later that year, she separated from Rivera. During this time, she painted one of her most famous works, *The Two Fridas* (1939). The painting is believed to depict the "unloved" and "loved" versions of Frida.

Oddly, Frida and Rivera remarried in 1940, and yet the couple continued to lead largely separate lives. By 1941, though her health remained frail, her work gained popularity both within Mexico and beyond it.

In 1944, Frida painted *The Broken Column*, which depicted her physical struggles. Around this time, she had several surgeries and wore special corsets to try to fix her back. She also sought treatments for her chronic physical pain, but with little success.

Deteriorating Health and Death

Her health issues became nearly all-consuming in 1950. After being diagnosed with gangrene in her right foot, she underwent several surgeries. Also, due to gangrene, her right leg below the knee had to be amputated. Despite these physical challenges, she continued to paint and even attended on a four-poster bed her first solo exhibition in Mexico in 1953. In her last self-portrait, she looks like a withered flower.

Her final public appearance was during a demonstration against the U.S. backed overthrow of President Jacobo Arbenz of Guatemala, on July 2. About a week after her 47th birthday, Frida died on July 13, 1954 at her beloved Blue House. Three years later, after her death, Rivera too passed away. Before his death, he donated the Blue House and today, it is a museum that holds many of Frida's paintings.

Fast Facts

Born:	July 6, 1907
Place of Birth:	Coyoacán, Mexico City, Mexico
Known for:	Painting
Movement:	Surrealism, Magic Realism
Famous works:	The Two Fridas, The Wounded Deer

The Two Fridas

Giovanni Lorenzo Bernini

Born in Naples in 1598, Italian architect and sculptor Giovanni Lorenzo Bernini is credited with creating the Baroque style of sculpture (represented by complex architectural plan shapes, grandeur, drama and contrast, curvaceousness, twisting elements and gilded statuary). He contributed to a number of landmarks in Rome, including *St. Peter's Basilica* and the *Fountain of the Four Rivers*.

Early Life

Giovanni Lorenzo Bernini was the son of the sculptor Pietro Bernini. When he was still a child, Bernini was taught his first art lessons by his father. He made such great progress that he successfully completed an angel's head in marble by the age of 10. In 1608, he accompanied his father to Rome. There he grabbed attention due to his well-developed artistic talent at such a young age. While in Rome, he attended an art class and made many busts, including one of the pope.

Fame and Fortune

Bernini's perfection and mastery while crafting stone gained him fame at a young age. He carved at great speed without requiring calculations and brought life to stone. With his special surface design, which reflected the links between the skin and the underlying muscles and bones in its most minute detail, he managed to make the stone appear smoother than ever before.

Between 1618 and 1625, he produced the famous mythological groups of sculptures—*Aeneas, Anchises and Ascanius*, *Pluto and Persephone*, *Apollo and Daphne* and *David* for Cardinal Scipione Borghese. These works are still admired today. Unlike sculptures made by other artists, the ones made by Bernini focus on specific points in the narrative story which they depict—Aeneas and his family fleeing the burning Troy; the instant that Pluto finally grasps the hunted Persephone; the precise moment that Apollo sees his beloved Daphne as she begins her transformation into a tree. All these are powerful moments in each story. Bernini's *David* too depicts a crucial moment where David is in combat with the giant. Bernini's *David* has twisted his body in preparation to send a catapult towards the giant Goliath. Bernini had created all these sculptures with a specific moment from the narrative in his mind and these leave a powerful impact on the viewer.

Bernini had manifold artistic skills and a highly inventive talent, which he employed in architecture with equal dedication and great success. The nearly unbroken favour by the pope helped Bernini to get important commissions. He was thus supported in such a manner that throughout his lifetime he was able to contribute and undertake the greatest artistic undertakings of the Roman court.

In 1629, Bernini became the master builder of the Church of St. Peter in Rome—even though he had never been

Apollo and Daphne

trained as an architect—and started to build the bell towers on both sides of the facade, which were later taken down.

Despite his numerous works, his chief works include the mighty colonnades, which were built in 1667 and which enclose the square in front of the church of St. Peter, offering a magnificent and impressive view. In this manner, Bernini left a decisive mark in his architectural work in Rome. Alongside his sculptures and architectural work, Bernini produced over 150 paintings depicting biblical and secular stories and the world of mythology—pictures, which are admired all over the world particularly in Italy.

Fountains in Rome

Bernini, along with his renowned sculptures, also created a number of fountains based on the Baroque style. His fountains were public works, which were at the same time also papal monuments. Fountains which Bernini had created include the Fountain of the Triton, or Fontana del Tritone, and the Barberini Fountain of the Bees, the Fontana delle Api. The Fountain of the Four Rivers or Fontana dei Quattro Fiumi, in the Piazza Navona is a masterpiece of spectacle

Ecstasy of Saint Teresa

created by the master craftsman. In 1653, he created the statue of the Moor in La Fontana del Moro, which is placed in the Piazza Navona.

Later Years and Death

In his later years, Bernini enjoyed an almost princely acclaim, soon received the Cross of the Order of Christ, and was a favourite of all the popes that reigned during his lifetime. He was so popular that the pope himself and the Swedish Queen Christine, who stayed in Rome, often visited him in his apartment with their court.

Bernini married at the age of 41, to a 22-year-old Roman woman, Caterina Tezio. Together they bore eleven children. His youngest son, Domenico Bernini, became his father's first biographer. Owning one of his works was a matter of honour and the aristocracy wanted to own his works. It was only Pope Innocence X who denied Bernini his goodwill. At that time, Giovanni Lorenzo Bernini's reputation as one of the greatest artists of his time was so strong that he received large private commissions, including that for the interior design of the Cornaro Chapel in Rome (1645-53), which gave rise to the famous *St. Theresa in Ecstasy*.

In 1664, at the age of 66, Bernini travelled to Paris to refurbish the Louvre. In 1680, when he died, he left a legacy of great architecture that led to his eternal fame.

Fast Facts

Born:	Dec. 7, 1598
Place of Birth:	Naples, Italy
Known for:	Sculpture, paintings, architecture
Movement:	Baroque style
Famous works:	David, Ecstasy of Saint Teresa

David

Henri Rousseau

Myself: Portrait – Landscape

Henri Rousseau, while working as a toll collector in Paris, taught himself to paint and later exhibited his work almost annually from 1886 until the end of his life. Despite his connections with other artists and dealers, he never earned profits from his paintings. However, works like *The Dream*, *The Sleeping Gypsy* and *Carnival Evening* influenced many artists.

Early Life and Work

Henri Julien Félix Rousseau was born into a middle-class family. After attending school, he worked for a lawyer and later got himself enlisted in the army. However, he never saw combat. In 1868, Rousseau left the army and moved to Paris where he began working as a toll collector.

Rousseau as Artist

Even while working as a toll collector, Rousseau would paint in his spare time. He never had a formal training in art. Instead, he would learn by copying paintings in the art museums of Paris and by sketching in the city's botanical gardens and natural history museums.

Perhaps because he had not studied art, he managed to develop his own personal style. His portraits and landscapes often reflect a childlike or "naïve" quality, since he had not learned anatomy or perspective. The vivid colours, ambiguous spaces, non-realistic scale and dramatic intensity used in his works, lend them a dreamlike quality.

Many of Rousseau's signature paintings depict human figures or wild animals in jungle-like settings. The first of these works was *Tiger in a Tropical Storm*, painted in 1891.

'Le Douanier' and the Avant-Garde

Although Rousseau's art was not understood or accepted by the conservative, official art world of Paris, he was able to showcase his work in annual exhibitions organized by the Société des Artistes Indépendants. He submitted works there, and gained appreciation until the last years of his life and garnered appreciation from artists like Camille Pissarro and Paul Signac.

In 1893, after retiring from his job as a toll collector, Rousseau devoted all his time to art. That year, he met writer Alfred Jarry, who introduced him to members of the Parisian artistic and literary avant-garde, including Pablo Picasso, Guillaume Apollinaire, Max Jacob and Marie Laurencin, all of whom became great admirers of his art. During this time, he also formed business alliances with important dealers but despite his connections, he made little money from his works.

Exotic Landscape with Lion and Lioness in Africa

Death and Artistic Legacy

Rousseau died on September 2, 1910, in Paris. His work continued to influence other artists, from his friend Picasso to Fernand Léger, Max Ernst and the Surrealists. Today, his paintings are displayed in museums around the world.

Boy on the Rocks

Fast Facts

Born:	May 21, 1844
Place of Birth:	Laval, Mayenne
Known for:	Painting
Movement:	Post-impressionism, naïve art
Famous works:	The Sleeping Gypsy, Boy on the Rocks

M.F. Husain

M. F. Husain was born to a Sulaymani Bohra family in Maharashtra, India. He picked up taste in art as he studied calligraphy at a Madrasa in Baroda. He was primarily self-taught. During his early years, he painted cinema posters in Bombay (now Mumbai). However, whenever he got a chance, he travelled to Gujarat to paint landscapes—a subject close to his heart.

The year 1947 saw many young artists across the country trying to break away from the traditions established by the Bengal school of art and encouraging an Indian avant-garde. In order to do so, the artists formed The Progressive Artist's Group in Bombay. Husain became part of this group. Later, he had his first solo exhibit as an artist in 1952 in Zurich. He also exhibited his works at the India House in New York in 1964. In 1966, in recognition for his contribution to art, he was awarded the prestigious Padma Shri, the fourth highest civilian award in the Republic of India.

Painting Career and Controversies

In 1967, Husain tried his skills in film making and made his first film, *Through the Eyes of a Painter*. It was shown at the Berlin International Film Festival, where it won the Golden Bear short film award. Later, for his varied works, Husain was also awarded the Padma Bhushan (1973) and the Padma Vibhushan (1991).

Although a popular artist, he triggered criticism

for his treatment of sensitive subject matter. For instance, his painting of Hindu goddesses as nudes hurt the religious sentiments of Hindu nationalist groups, which led to nationwide protests. The paintings in question were created in 1970 but did not become an issue until 1996, when they were printed in *Vichar Mimansa*, a Hindi monthly magazine. As many as eight criminal complaints were filed against him. Though the court dismissed the complaints, the fundamentalists continued to protest against him and vandalized his works. Amid protests for his work, he found himself in another controversy where in an advertisement, he had drawn a nude portrait of Mother India posing across a map of India with the names of Indian States on several parts of her body. Amid soaring protests, Husain made an apology and promised to withdraw the painting from an auction.

Hailed as the "Picasso of India", Husain also produced and directed several films, including *Gaja Gamini* (2000), where the protagonist portrays the various forms and manifestations of womanhood. He then directed *Meenaxi: A Tale of Three Cities*. The film was pulled out of cinemas a day after some Muslim organizations raised objections to one of the songs in it. Despite these setbacks, the film went on to win various critics awards.

In 2006, Husain went into a self-imposed exile. During this time, he switched his

Bharatmata

stayed between Doha and London. He also gained the citizenship of Qatar. In Qatar, he principally worked on two large projects—one on the history of Arab civilization, and another on the history of Indian civilization.

Husain spent the last years of his life living in Doha and London, staying away from India, but always longing to return. He died, aged 95, following a heart attack.

Fast Facts

Born:	Sep. 17, 1915
Place of Birth:	Pandharpur, Maharashtra, India
Known for:	Painting, drawing, writing, film making
Movement:	Progressive art group
Famous works:	Bharatmata, Man, Vishwamitra, and Passage Through Human Space

Leonardo da Vinci

Born in Vinci, Italy, Leonardo da Vinci was concerned with the laws of science and nature, which greatly formed his work as a painter, sculptor, inventor and draftsman. His ideas and body of work—which includes *Virgin of the Rocks*, *The Last Supper*, *Leda and the Swan* and *Mona Lisa*—have influenced countless artists and made Vinci among the greatest of the Italian Renaissance artists and perhaps the best in the world.

Humble Beginnings

Leonardo da Vinci was born to a respected notary and a young peasant woman. His parents were not married. Vinci was raised by his father, Ser Piero and his stepmothers. At the young age of 14, Vinci began apprenticeship with Verrocchio, an artist. For six years, he learned a wide breadth of technical skills, including metalworking, leather arts, carpentry, drawing and sculpting. He was only 20, when he qualified as a master artist and he even established his own workshop.

'The Last Supper'

In 1482, Lorenzo de' Medici, a man from a prominent Italian family, commissioned Vinci to create a silver lyre and bring it to Ludovico il Moro, the Duke of Milan, as a gesture of peace. Vinci did so and then wrote a letter to Moro, describing how his engineering and artistic talents could be of great service to Moro's court. His letter endeared him to Moro and Vinci was commissioned several works. It was during this time that he had also painted *The Last Supper*.

Mona Lisa

The Last Supper is said to have been started by da Vinci around 1495. It was commissioned as part of the renovations that was thought of for the church and its convent buildings. The painting is located on the end wall of the dining hall at the monastery of Santa Maria delle Grazie in Milan, Italy. The painting, a masterpiece in its own right, shows the scene of the last meal that Jesus partook with his disciples. Vinci represented the precise moment when Jesus announced to his disciples that one among them was soon to betray him. In the painting, Vinci has captured the expression of each disciple, which is a mix of varied degrees of anger and shock. Interestingly, the apostles can be identified from the manuscript where Vinci had written their names.

'Mona Lisa'

Vinci's most well-known, and arguably the most famous, painting in the world, *Mona Lisa*, was a privately commissioned work. It was completed sometime between 1505 and 1507.

It has been said that the original Mona Lisa had jaundice, that she was pregnant, and that she wasn't actually a woman at all, but a man in drag. Based on accounts from an early biographer, the *painting depicts* Lisa Gioconda, the real-life wife of a merchant, but even this version is far from certain. The most striking feature of the painting is the elusive smile on the woman's face. For da Vinci, the *Mona Lisa* was forever a work in progress. He never delivered the painting to the commissioner, keeping it with him till his last day. Today, the *Mona Lisa* is considered a priceless treasure and hangs in heavy security in the Louvre Museum in Paris.

Drawings

Vinci was not only a creative painter but also prolific draftsperson. He kept detailed journals which were full of small sketches and detailed drawings, recording almost anything that caught his attention. Several paintings accompanied his journals. These paintings have been thought as preparatory to some of his works, such as *The Adoration of the Magi*, *The Virgin of the Rocks* and *The Last Supper*.

Among his famous drawings are the *Vitruvian Man*, which is a study of the

The Last Supper

proportions of the human body, *Star of Bethlehem* and a large drawing in black chalk of *The Virgin and Child with St. Anne* and *St. John the Baptist*. Several of his other drawings are considered caricatures as they appear to be based on his observation of live models.

Renaissance Man

Da Vinci has been called a genius and the archetypal Renaissance Man. His talents inarguably extended far beyond his artistic works. Like many leaders of Renaissance humanism, he refused to see a divide between science and art. His observations and inventions were recorded in 13,000 pages of notes and drawings, including designs for flying machines, plant studies, war machinery, anatomy and architecture. His ideas were mainly theoretical explanations, laid out in exacting detail, but they were rarely experimental. His drawings of a fetus in womb, the heart and vascular system, sex organs, and other bone and muscular structures are some of the first on human organ detailing.

One of Vinci's last commissioned works was a mechanical lion that could walk and open its chest to reveal a bouquet of lilies. The famous artist died in Amboise, France, on May 2, 1519.

The Virgin and Child with St. Anne

Fast Facts

Born:	April 15, 1452
Place of Birth:	Vinci, Republic of Florence
Known for:	Polymath
Movement:	High Renaissance
Famous works:	Mona Lisa, The Last Supper

Michelangelo Buonarroti

Michelangelo Buonarroti was born in Caprese near Florence (Italy), where his father was the local magistrate. He became an apprentice to a painter before he started to study in the sculpture gardens of the powerful Medici family, the leading patron of the arts in Florence. What followed was a remarkable career as an artist in the Italian Renaissance. His works include world-famous statues like *David* and *Pieta*, and the ceiling paintings of Rome's Sistine Chapel, including the *Last Judgment*.

Early Life

Born to a family of moderate means, Buonarroti rose to become one of the most famous artists of the Italian Renaissance. Sometime after his birth, he was placed with a family of stonecutters due to his mother's illness.

While growing up, Buonarroti showed little interest in studies and would instead spend time watching the painters at nearby churches. He imbibed all that he saw there. It may have been his grammar school friend, Francesco Granacci, six years his senior, who introduced him to painter Domenico Ghirlandaio. Buonarroti's father realized early that his son was interested in arts, so he had him become an apprentice to a fashionable Florentine painter. Buonarroti was only 13 year old at that time. As an apprentice, he was exposed to the technique of fresco paintings (a technique of mural painting executed upon freshly laid plaster).

Buonarroti spent only a year at the workshop when an extraordinary opportunity opened to him. At the recommendation of Ghirlandaio, he moved into the palace of the powerful Medici family, to study classical sculpture in the Medici gardens. During these years, he was introduced to the elite society and he also studied under the respected sculptor Bertoldo di Giovanni, who exposed Buonarroti to prominent poets, scholars and learned humanists. These combined influences laid the groundwork for his distinctive style and presentation of reality combined with lyrical beauty.

Early Success and Influences

Soon, due to political strife, Buonarroti fled to Bologna, where he continued his studies. He returned to Florence in 1495 to begin work as a sculptor. After tasting great success in Florence, he moved to Rome where he lived and worked for the rest of his life.

The 'Pieta' and the 'David'

Not long after his relocation to Rome in 1498, his fledgling career was bolstered

David

by cardinal, Jean Bilhères de Lagraulas. *Buonarroti's Pietà*, a sculpture of Mary holding the dead Jesus on her lap, was finished in less than a year. At six feet wide and nearly as tall, the statue has been moved five times and presently is placed in St. Peter's Basilica in the Vatican City.

Carved from a single piece of Carrara marble, the fluidity of the fabric, positions of the subjects and "movement" of the skin of the Piet—meaning "pity" or "compassion"—inspires awe. Today, the *Pietà* remains an incredibly revered work of art around the world. Buonarroti was just 25 years old at the time of its completion.

By now, he had become an art star. He then was commissioned for a statue of *David*, and in time, he turned the 17-foot piece of marble into a dominating figure.

Art and Architecture

Several commissions followed, including painting of the ceiling of Sistine Chapel. The project fuelled Buonarroti's imagination, and the original plan for 12 apostles morphed into more than 300 figures on the ceiling of the sacred space. Dismissing all his assistants, he alone painted the ceiling and jealously guarded it until it was revealed to public eye. The work is an example of high renaissance art, which incorporates the Christian symbology, prophecy and humanist principles. Though he continued to sculpt and paint throughout his life, the physical rigour of painting the chapel took its toll on him and he turned his focus towards architecture.

He went on to design the Medici Chapel and the Laurentian Library. Later, he was also appointed as the chief architect of St. Peter's Basilica in 1546.

The Sistine Chapel Ceiling

Buonarroti is singly credited with the painting of the ceiling at Sistine Chapel in Rome. Despite several setbacks, he completed painting the ceiling in four years singlehandedly. The centre of the ceiling depicts many scenes from *The Genesis*, including scenes from the creation, to the fall, to Noah's deluge. Various prophets, who had foretold about

Plafond de la Chapelle Sixtine, Vatican

the coming of the Messiah, adorn the sides of the vast ceiling.

Interestingly, in the beginning, Buonarroti was reluctant to take up the project but later he was able to convince Pope Julius II to let him compose the ceiling now that he had good understanding of the theme. When the ceiling was complete, it left many awestruck. Even today, the painting continues to inspire many artists around the world.

Death and Legacy

Following a brief illness, Buonarroti Michelangelo died on February 18, 1564—just weeks before his 89th birthday—at his home in Macel de'Corvi, Rome. Unlike many artists, he achieved great fame and wealth during his lifetime. He also had two biographies written on him during his lifetime. Appreciation of his artistic mastery has endured for centuries, and his name has become synonymous with the best of the Italian Renaissance.

Fast Facts

Born:	March 6, 1475
Place of Birth:	Caprese, Republic of Florence
Known for:	Sculpture, painting, architecture
Movement:	High Renaissance
Famous works:	David, Sistine Chapel ceiling

Pietà

Oscar Claude Monet

One of the most famous painters in the history of art and a leading figure in the Impressionist Movement, Oscar Claude Monet was born in Paris, France. Monet's father, Adolphe, worked in his family's shipping business, while his mother, Louise, a trained singer, took care of the family.

In 1845, at the age of 5, Monet moved with his family to Le Havre, a port town in the Normandy region. At an early age, Monet developed a love for drawing. He filled his schoolbooks with sketches of people, including caricatures of his teachers. While his mother supported his artistic endeavours, Monet's father wanted him to be part of the family business.

In the community, Monet became well known for his caricatures and for drawing many of the town's residents. After meeting Eugene Boudin, a local landscape artist, Monet started to explore the natural world in his work. Boudin introduced him to painting outdoors, which would later become the cornerstone of Monet's work. In 1857, post his mother's death Monet dropped out of school and went to live with his aunt, Marie-Jeanne Lecadre.

In Pursuit of Art

In 1859, Monet decided to move to Paris to pursue his art. In the beginning he used to visit the Louvre Museum, where he saw various artists copying the masters. Monet did no such thing. In June 1861, he joined the First Regiment of African Light Cavalry in Algeria. He had signed to serve them for seven years. However, two years later, he contacted typhoid fever, and his aunt intervened to get him out of the army. She, however, had to ensure them that Monet would complete an art course at an art school. At the art school, however, Monet learnt nothing new. Soon after, he met Charles Gleyre in Paris and became his student.

Through Gleyre, Monet met several other artists. Monet liked to work outdoors and was sometimes accompanied by Renoir, Sisley and Bazille on these painting sojourns. Together they shared new approaches to art. They began painting the effects of light en plein air (the act of painting outdoors, where the painter reproduces the actual visual conditions seen at the time of the painting) with broken colour and rapid brush strokes. This technique later came to be known as Impressionism. Monet won acceptance to the Salon of 1865, an annual juried art show in Paris. The show chose two of his paintings, which were marine landscapes. Though Monet's works received critical praise, he still struggled financially. The following year, Monet was selected again to participate in the Salon. This time, the show officials chose a landscape and a portrait *Camille* (or also called *Woman in Green*), which featured his lover and future wife, Camille Doncieux. After getting married in 1870, Monet and his wife continued to travel. At one point in time, Monet even attempted suicide due to his monetary woes.

However, things took a turn when Louis-Joachim Guadibert became a patron of Monet's work, which enabled the artist to continue his work and care for his family.

The Master of Light and Colour

The society's April 1874 exhibition proved to be revolutionary. At the exhibition, Monet presented four oil paintings and seven pastels. One of Monet's most noted works in the show, *Impression, Sunrise* (1873), depicted Le

Poplars (Autumn)

Havre's harbour in a morning fog. Critics used the title to name the distinct group of artists "Impressionists," saying that their work seemed more like sketches than finished paintings. Interestingly, many of the paintings exhibited were also sold at good prices.

Although it was meant to be derogatory, the term seemed fitting. Monet sought to capture the essence of the natural world using strong colours and bold, short brushstrokes; he and his contemporaries were turning away from the blended colours and evenness of classical art. Monet began to exhibit with the Impressionists after their first show in 1874, and continued into the 1880s.

Monet's personal life was marked by hardship around this time. His wife died, which was a terrible loss to both Monet and their two children. Monet gained financial and critical success during the late 1880s and 1890s, and started the serial paintings for which he would become well known. In Giverny, he loved to paint outdoors in the gardens that he helped create there. The water lilies found in the pond had a particular appeal for him, and he painted several series of them throughout the rest of his life. Along with these paintings, he also painted several similar looking scenes of the French countryside in order to capture the effect of light and shade and the changing of seasons.

In the early 1890s, he rented a room across from the Rouen Cathedral in northwestern France, and painted a series of works that focused on the structure of the cathedral. Different paintings showed the building in morning light, midday, grey weather and more; this repetition was a result of Monet's deep fascination with the effects of light.

In 1912, he developed cataracts in his right eye. Meanwhile, in the art world, Monet was out of step with the

Impression, Sunrise

avant-garde. But there was still a great deal of interest in Monet's work. During this period, he began a final series of 12 waterlily paintings commissioned by the Orangerie des Tuileries, a museum in Paris. This project consumed much of Monet's later years. During this time, he also underwent surgery for his cataract in 1923.

Later Years

As he experienced in other points in his life, Monet struggled with depression in his later years. Despite his feelings of despair, he continued working on his paintings until his final days. Monet died on December 5, 1926, at his home in Giverny. He once wrote, "My only merit lies in having painted directly in front of nature, seeking to render my impressions of the most fleeting effects." Most art historians believe that Monet accomplished much more than this as his paintings had shaken off the conventions of the past.

Monet's Methods of Painting

Monet has often been described as "the driving force behind Impressionism." The effects of light on various objects and the combination of various colours are crucial to the understanding of the Impressionist painters. All through his career as an Impressionist painter, Monet continued to understand this method. Even in his last years, he continued to visit art galleries and familiarized himself with the work of older painters. Monet thought in terms of colours and shapes rather than scenes and objects. He painted same scenes which showed the effect of light on the same objects. He also studied the effects on objects due to the change in seasons and weather. In simpler terms, his technique focused on light and its effects rather than on the objects. He began using this technique in the 1880s and continued to work on it until the end of his life in 1926.

Fast Facts

Born:	Nov. 14, 1840
Place of Birth:	Paris, France
Known for:	Paintings
Movement:	Impressionism
Famous works:	Water Lilies, Poplars

Woman in a Garden

Pablo Picasso

Picasso was born to Doña Maria Picasso y Lopez and Don José Ruiz Blasco, a painter and art teacher. A serious and prematurely world-weary child, the young Picasso possessed a pair of piercing, watchful black eyes. "When I was a child, my mother said to me, 'If you become a soldier, you'll be a general. If you become a monk, you'll end up as the pope,'" he recalled once. "Instead, I became a painter and wound up as Picasso."

Though he was a relatively poor student, Picasso displayed a prodigious talent for drawing at a very young age. Picasso's father started teaching him how to draw and paint when he was a child, and by the time he was 13, his skill level had surpassed his father's.

In 1895, when Picasso was 14 years old, he was admitted to Barcelona's School of Fine Arts but he attended less of it due to their strict rules. Instead, he sat drawing street scenes he observed. In 1897, Picasso moved to Madrid to attend the Royal Academy of San Fernando. But again, he remained mostly outside for he disliked their techniques of teaching. This time, he wandered the city and painted gypsies, beggars and prostitutes, among other subjects.

In 1899, Picasso moved back to Barcelona and started to experiment and innovate in his work of art. In Barcelona, he met his first Parisian friend, journalist and poet Max

Jacob, who helped Picasso learn French and told him about French literature. Soon they started sharing an apartment. These were times of severe poverty, cold and desperation. Picasso burned much of his work to keep the small room warm. During the first five months of 1901, Picasso lived in Madrid, where he along with his friend Francisco de Asís Soler founded the magazine *Arte Joven (Young Art)*. They could only publish five issues of the magazine. While Soler solicited articles, Picasso illustrated the journal, mostly depicting the state of the poor. It was also while making cartoons for the magazine that Picasso began signing his works.

Blue Period: 'Blue Nude,' 'La Vie' and Other Works

At the turn of the 20th century, Pablo Picasso moved to Paris, to open his own studio. Art critics and historians typically break Picasso's adult career into distinct periods, the first of which lasted from 1901 to 1904 and is called his "Blue Period," after the colour that dominated nearly all of Picasso's paintings over these years. In this period, he painted scenes of poverty, isolation and anguish, almost exclusively in shades of blue and green. Picasso's most famous paintings from the Blue Period include *Blue Nude*, *La Vie* and *The Old Guitarist*, all three of which were completed in 1903. Blindness is a recurring theme in Picasso's paintings of this time.

Rose Period: 'Gertrude Stein,' 'Two Nudes' and More

By 1905, Picasso's depression had faded and he was madly in love with a beautiful model, Fernande Olivier, he was newly prosperous thanks to the generous patronage of art dealer Ambroise Vollard. The artistic manifestation of Picasso's improved spirits was the introduction of warmer colours—including beiges, pinks and reds—in what is known as his "Rose Period" (1904-06). Picasso's paintings from this period focus on harlequins, acrobats and people that lived and worked in a circus. His paintings of this period also have a mood of optimism. Also during this period, his works started to find art collectors. His most famous paintings from these years include "Family at Saltimbanques" (1905),

Couple, le baiser

"Gertrude Stein" (1905-06) and "Two Nudes" (1906).

Break into Cubism

In 1907, Pablo Picasso produced a painting unlike anything he or anyone else had ever painted before—a work that would profoundly influence the direction of art in the 20th century: *Les Demoiselles d'Avignon*, a chilling depiction of five nude prostitutes, abstracted and distorted with sharp geometric features and stark blotches of blues, greens and greys. Today, *Les Demoiselles d'Avignon* is considered the precursor and inspiration of Cubism, an artistic style pioneered by Picasso and his friend and fellow painter, Georges Braque.

In Cubist paintings, objects are broken apart and reassembled in an abstracted form, highlighting their geometric shapes and depicting them from multiple, simultaneous viewpoints in order to create collage-like effects. At once destructive and creative, Cubism shocked, appalled and fascinated the art world. The new style was a revolutionary movement.

Classical Period

The outbreak of World War I ushered in the next great change in Picasso's art. He grew more somber and, once again, became preoccupied with the depiction of reality. His works between 1918 and 1927 are categorized as part of his "Classical Period," a brief return to Realism in a career otherwise dominated by experimentation.

Surrealism

From 1927 onward, Picasso became caught up in a new philosophical and cultural movement known as Surrealism, the artistic manifestation of which was a product of his own Cubism.

Picasso's most well-known Surrealist painting "*Guernica*" was completed in 1937. Painted in black, white and greys, the work is a Surrealist testament to the horrors of war.

Guernica is a large oil painting, which Picasso had completed in 1937. Black, white and grey are the only three colours used in the painting. The painting is a moving and powerful depiction of war and the suffering which it brings. It is believed to be Picasso's response to the bombing of Guernica, a village in northern

Buste d'Homme

Spain. The painting has helped bring attention to the suffering, hopelessness, devastation and waste which any war brings.

'Self Portrait Facing Death' and Other Later Works

In the aftermath of World War II, Picasso became more overtly political. By this point in his life, he was also an international celebrity, the world's most famous living artist.

In contrast to the dazzling complexity of Synthetic Cubism, Picasso's later paintings display simple, childlike imagery and crude technique. Picasso created the epitome of his later work, *Self Portrait Facing Death*, using pencil and crayon, a year before his death. The expression in his eyes, capturing a lifetime of wisdom, fear and uncertainty, is the unmistakable work of a master.

Death and Legacy

Picasso continued to create art and maintain an ambitious schedule in his later years. He died on April 8, 1973, at the age of 91, in Mougins, France. Inarguably one of the most celebrated and influential painters of the 20th century, Picasso continues to be revered for his technical mastery, creativity and vision. His ability to drastically change his styles makes it seem that these works have been made by several artists rather than by one.

Fast Facts

Born:	Oct. 25, 1881
Place of Birth:	Málaga, Spain
Known for:	Painting, printmaking, ceramics, writing, stage designing
Movement:	Cubism, Surrealism
Famous works:	The Weeping Woman, Les Demoiselles d'Avignon

Femme au costume turc dans un fauteuil

Raphael Sanzio

Italian Renaissance painter and architect Raphael Sanzio was born in Urbino, Italy. His father Giovanni was a painter for the Duke of Urbino. Giovanni taught the young Sanzio basic painting techniques and exposed him to the principles of humanistic philosophy at the Duke of Urbino's court.

In 1494, when Sanzio was just 11 years old, he lost his father. Sanzio then took over the daunting task of managing his father's workshop. His success at painting soon surpassed his father's reputation and Sanzio fame spread as one of the finest painters in town.

In 1500, a master painter named Pietro Vannunci, invited Raphael Sanzio to become his apprentice in Perugia, in the Umbria region of central Italy. In Perugia, Perugino was working on frescoes at the Collegio del Cambia and Raphael Sanzio assisted him in his works. The apprenticeship lasted four years and provided Raphael Sanzio with the opportunity to gain both knowledge and hands-on experience. During this period, he developed his own unique painting style, as is exhibited in his works like *The Mond Crucifixion, The Three Graces, The Knight's Dream,* and the Oddi altarpiece, *Marriage of the Virgin.*

Paintings

In 1504, Sanzio left his apprenticeship with Perugino and moved to Florence, where he was influenced by the work of art giants. By closely studying the details of their work, he developed a more intricate and expressive style of his own. From 1504 through 1507, Sanzio produced a series of "Madonnas," which were influenced by da Vinci's works. In 1507, he created his most ambitious work in Florence, *The Entombment*.

Sanzio moved to Rome in 1508 to paint in the Vatican "Stanze" ("Room"), under Pope Julius II's patronage. From 1509 to 1511, he toiled over what became Italian High Renaissance's most highly regarded fresco cycles, located in the Vatican's Stanza della Segnatura. In the fresco cycle, Sanzio expressed the humanistic philosophy that he had learned as a boy.

In the years to come, he painted another fresco cycle for the Vatican. During the same time, the ambitious painter produced a successful series of "Madonna" paintings including the famed *Madonna of the Chair* and *Sistine Madonna*.

The Transfiguration

The Transfiguration is the last painting which Sanzio painted at the time of his death. Due to his untimely death, the painting remained incomplete. In this painting, Sanzio represents two different happenings from *the Bible*. In the first part, the transfiguration of Christ itself takes place as Moses and Elijah appear

Transfiguration

before the transfigured Christ. Peter, James and John, the three apostles, are shown looking on. In the second part, the apostles are shown having failed to cure a boy who has been possessed by demons. And so the Apostles await the arrival of Christ. As Christ appears, he performs a miracle and the child gets cured. By showing the two scenes together, Sanzio has put on record the healing power of the transfigured Christ. The painting is considered a fine example of both Mannerism and the style of Baroque painting.

The School of Athens

The School of Athens is the most famous fresco that has been painted by Sanzio. The painting is considered a masterpiece and a classical example of High Renaissance. Sanzio has painted every great Greek philosopher in the painting. The painting has a number of individuals and each one of them reflects a different emotion. Completed between 1509 and 1511, the painting was commissioned to decorate the walls of one of the rooms in the Vatican.

The School of Athens

Architecture

By 1514, Sanzio was quite popular with the church authorities and also otherwise. While he continued to accept commissions—including portraits of popes Julius II and Leo X—and his largest painting on canvas, *The Transfiguration*, he had by this time begun to work on architecture, especially for the church. Under this appointment, Sanzio created the design for a chapel in Sant'Eligio degli Orefici. He also designed Rome's Santa Maria del Popolo Chapel and an area within Saint Peter's new basilica. Interestingly, along with designing religious buildings, he also designed palaces.

Death and Legacy

On April 6, 1520, Raphael's 37th birthday, he died suddenly and unexpectedly of mysterious causes in Rome, Italy. He had been working on his largest painting on canvas, *The Transfiguration*, at the time of his death. When his funeral mass was held at the Vatican, his unfinished painting was placed on his coffin stand. Following his death, Raphael's movement toward Mannerism influenced painting styles in Italy's advancing Baroque period.

Fast Facts

Born:	April 6, 1483
Place of Birth:	Urbino, Marche, Italy
Known for:	Painting, architecture
Movement:	High Renaissance
Famous works:	The Madonna of the Meadow, The Transfiguration

The Engagement of Virgin Mary

Rembrandt Harmenszoon van Rijn

Born in Leiden, Netherlands in 1606, Rembrandt Harmenszoon van Rijn attended elementary school from 1612 to 1616, and then joined the Latin School in Leiden, where he partook in biblical studies and lessons on the classics.

From 1620 to 1624 or 1625, Rijn was trained as an artist under two masters—painter Jacob van Swanenburgh, with whom he studied for about three years understanding basic artistic skills, and Amsterdam's Pieter Lastman, who was a well-known history painter and who developed Rijn's skills in the genre. He also told him how to place biblical and historical figures in complex settings.

The Leiden Period

In 1625, Rembrandt settled back in Leiden, now a master in his own right, and over the next six years he laid the foundation for his life's work. It was during this time that Lastman's influence was most noticeable in his work, as in several instances Rijn deconstructed his former master's compositions and reassembled them into his own. Rijn's paintings created at this time were generally small but rich in detail. Religious and allegorical themes were prominent in his works. He also worked on his first etchings (1626) in Leiden, and his eventual international fame would rely on the widespread dissemination of these works. During these works, he has beautifully displayed the use of light and dark.

Rijn's style soon took an innovative turn involving his use of light. His new style left large areas of his paintings obscured in shadow; through his interpretation, illumination grew rapidly weaker as it extended into the painting, creating spots of brightness and pockets of deep darkness. In this vein, in 1629 Rijn completed *Judas Repentant* and *Returning the Pieces of Silver*, among others—works that further indicate his interest in the handling of light.

From 1628, he started taking apprentices.

The First Amsterdam Period (1631–1636)

In 1631, Rijn formed a business alliance with Hendrick Uylenburgh, an Amsterdam entrepreneur who had a workshop that created portraits and restored paintings, among other activities. During this time, Rijn began to paint dramatic, large-scale biblical and mythological scenes using his high-contrast method of light and dark, such as *The Blinding of Samson* (1636) and *Danaë* (1636).

He also painted numerous commissioned portraits with the help of various assistants.

The Storm on the Sea of Galilee

The Third Amsterdam Period (1643–1658)

In the 10 years following the unveiling of *The Night Watch*, Rijn's overall artistic output diminished drastically and he produced no painted portrait. Speculation about what happened after *The Night Watch* has contributed to the "Rembrandt myth," according to which the artist became largely misunderstood and was ignored. Often blamed for Rijn supposed downfall is the death of his wife and the supposed rejection of *The Night Watch* by those who commissioned it.

It has been put forth that Rijn's crisis may have been an artistic one—that he had seen his methods stretched to their practical limits. The variations in his few paintings from 1642 to 1652 might be seen as a sign that he was searching for a new way forward.

The Night Watch

The Night Watch was painted by Rijn in 1642. It is amongst the most famous paintings by the artist and represents the height of the Dutch Golden Age of painting. The painting is well known for its huge size, the beautiful use of light and shadow, and for the simple reason that the military battalion seems to be in motion, which is in contrast to the still paintings of a battalion.

With his clever use of light and shadow, Rijn makes sure that the viewer sees the three prime characters in the painting—the two gentlemen in the centre of the painting and the girl in the background

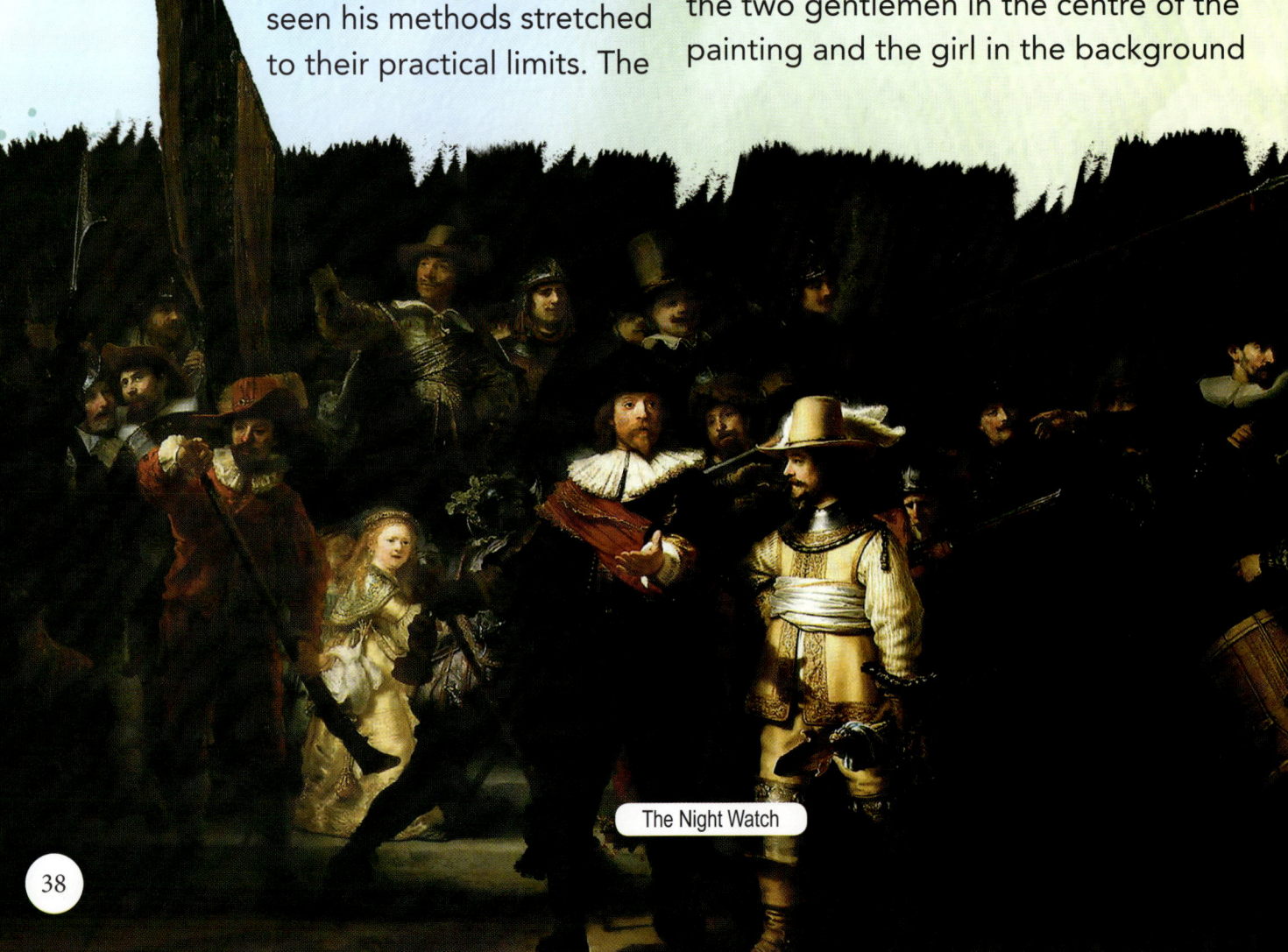

The Night Watch

at the centre. It is assumed that Rijn's painting has varied meanings and he had painted it to be thus to represent several things at the same time.

Belshazzar's Feast

Belshazzar's Feast, another of Rijn's paintings, is today housed in the National Gallery in London. This painting depicts the precise moment in the biblical story where during the feast of Belshazzar, the hand of God appears and writes about the downfall of Belshazzar on the wall. This story appears in the *Book of Daniel* in the *Old Testament*.

The inscription on the wall is an interesting element in this painting. Rijn had mistranscribed one of the characters while writing Hebrew and in order to fix his mistake, he had arranged the characters in columns instead of writing them from right to left as Hebrew is written.

Fast Facts

Born:	July 15, 1606
Place of Birth:	Leiden, Dutch Republic
Known for:	Painting, printmaking
Movement:	Dutch Golden Age, Baroque
Famous works:	The Night Watch, Belshazzar's Feast

Belshazzar's Feast

Salvador Dali

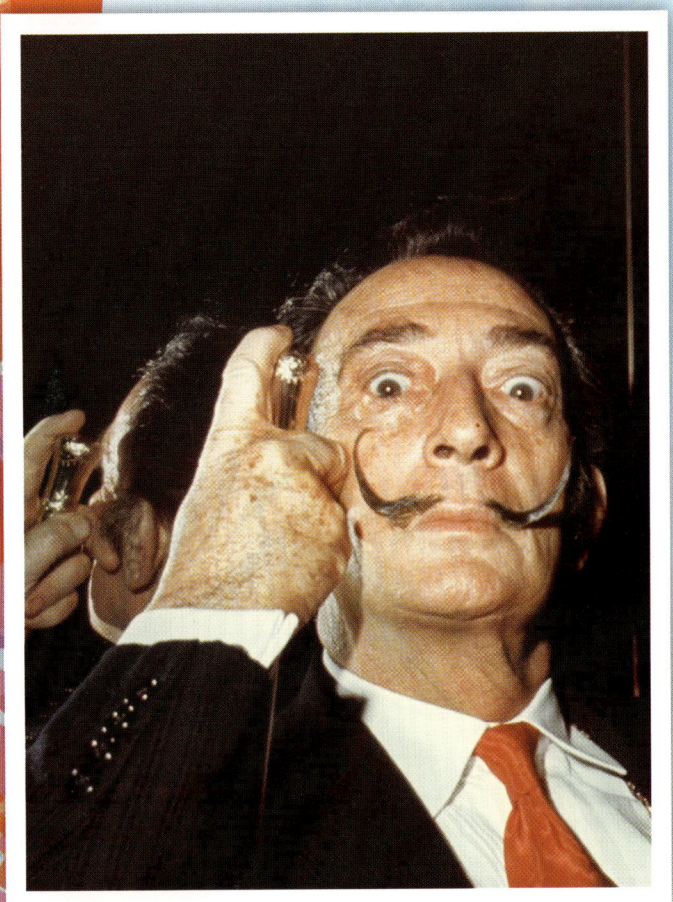

Salvador Dalí was born as Salvador Felipe Jacinto Dalí y Domenech. His father, Salvador Dalí y Cusi, was a middle-class lawyer and notary. Dalí father had a strict disciplinary approach to raising children. His mother, however, let him indulge in his eccentricities. He was an intelligent boy but his father did not approve of his irrational behaviour. However, both his parents knew that their son was inclined towards drawing and seeing his talent, encouraged him. His parents therefore built him an art studio before he entered art school. At the art school, he wasn't a serious student. He indulged in day dreams, wore odd clothing and kept his hair long.

After his first year at art school, he discovered modern painting in Cadaques while vacationing with his family. The following year, his father organized an exhibition of Dalí charcoal drawings in the family home. By 1919, the young artist had his first public exhibition, at the Municipal Theatre of Figueres.

In 1921, Dalí's mother, Felipa, died of breast cancer. Dalí was 16 years old at the time and was devastated by the loss.

Art School and Surrealism

In 1922, Dalí enrolled at the Academia de San Fernando in Madrid. He stayed at the school's student residence and soon brought his eccentricity to a new level—he grew his hair and dressed in the manner of 19th century style. During this time, he was influenced by several different artistic styles, including Metaphysics (use of representational but incongruous imagery to produce disquieting effects on the viewer) and Cubism (use of flat, two-dimensional surface of the picture plane).

In 1923, Dalí was suspended from the academy for criticizing his teachers and allegedly starting a riot among students. That same year, he was arrested and briefly imprisoned in Gerona for allegedly supporting the Separatist Movement. He returned to the academy in 1926, but was soon expelled for his behaviour.

Dalí soon began exploring many forms of art, including that of classical painters like Raphael, Bronzino and Diego Velázquez. He also dabbled in avant-garde art, which would later influence his work as an artist.

Between 1926 and 1929, Dalí made several trips to Paris, where he met influential painters and intellectuals such as Pablo Picasso, whom he revered. He also met several other painters and was introduced to Surrealism (use of the unconscious as a means to unlock the power of one's imagination). By this time, Dalí was working with styles of Impressionism, Futurism and Cubism. Dalí's paintings became associated with three general themes: 1) man's universe and sensations, 2) sexual symbolism, and 3) ideographic imagery.

This experimentation led to Dalí's first Surrealistic period in 1929. His oil paintings were small collages of his dream images. Dalí's major contribution to the Surrealist Movement was the

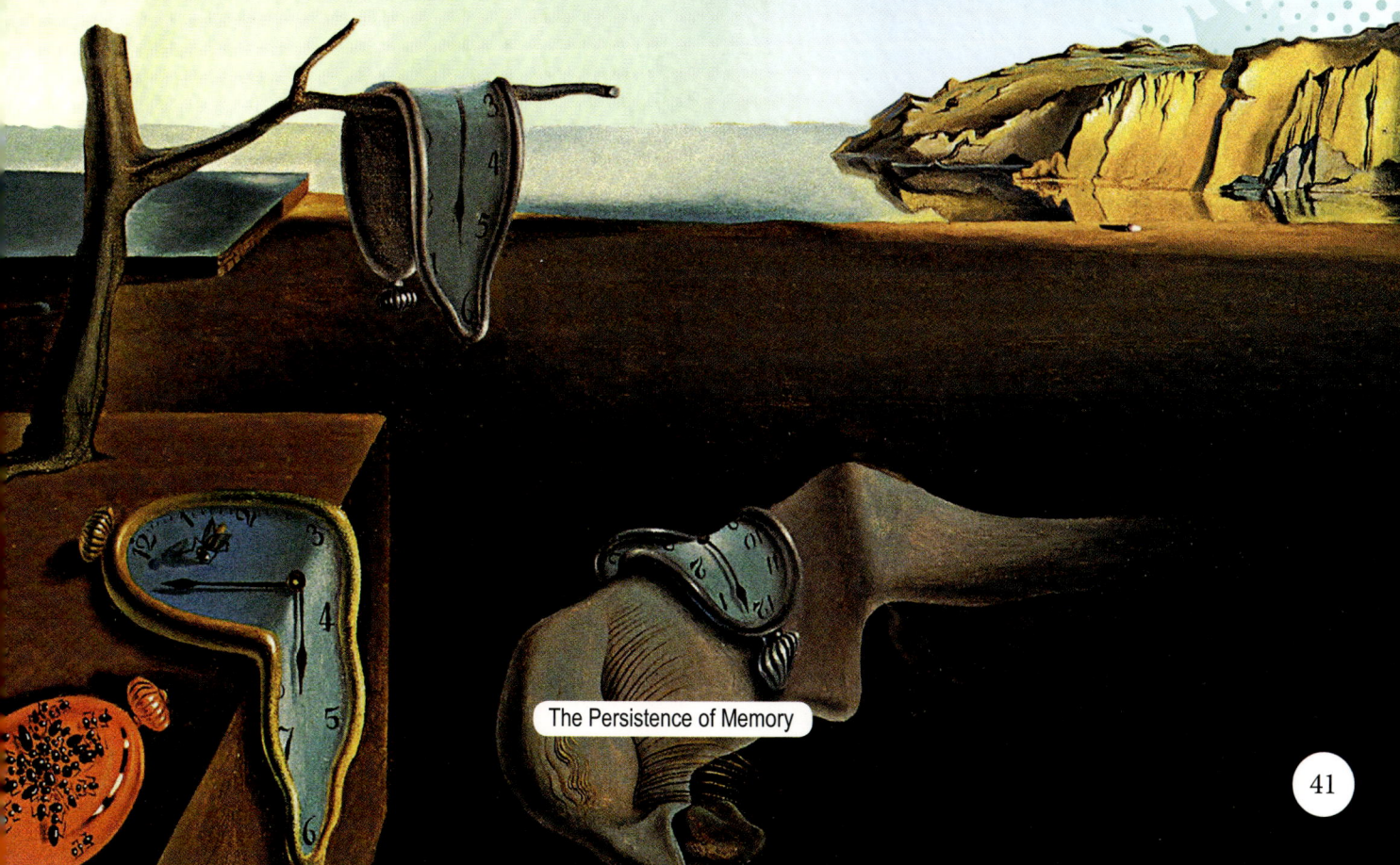

The Persistence of Memory

"paranoiac-critical method," where he created a reality from his dreams and thoughts, thus mentally changing reality to what he wanted it to be and not what it was. For Dalí, it became a way of life.

In 1929, Dalí expanded his artistic exploration into the world of film-making when he collaborated with Luis Buñuel on two films. Later, in 1945, Alfred Hitchcock also used his paintings, in a dream sequence, in one of his films.

In August 1929, Dalí met Elena Dmitrievna Diakonova, who helped to balance the creative forces in Dalí's life. With his wild expressions and fantasies, he wasn't capable of dealing with the business side of being an artist. Elena took care of his legal and financial matters. The two were married in a civil ceremony in 1934.

By 1930, Dalí had become a notorious figure of the Surrealist Movement. One of Dalí's most famous paintings produced at this time—and perhaps the best-known Surrealist work—was The Persistence of Memory (1931). The painting, sometimes called Soft Watches, shows melting pocket watches in a landscape setting. It is said that the painting conveys several ideas within the image—chiefly that time is not rigid and everything is destructible.

By the mid-1930s, Dalí became known for his colourful personality and his artwork.

The Dalí Theatre-Museum

During the late 40s through the 50s, Dalí painted a series of 19 large canvases that included scientific, historical or religious themes. He often called this period "Nuclear Mysticism." During this time, his artwork took on a technical brilliance combining meticulous detail with fantastic and limitless imagination. He would incorporate optical illusions, holography and geometry within his paintings. Much of his work contained images depicting divine geometry, the DNA, the Hyper Cube and religious themes of Chastity.

From 1960 to 1974, Dalí dedicated much of his time to creating the Teatro-Museo Dalí (Dalí Theatre-Museum) in Figueres. Located across the street from the Teatro-Museo Dalí is the Church of Sant Pere, where Dalí was baptized, had received his first communion and where his funeral would also take place.

The Teatro-Museo Dalí officially opened in 1974. It was built according to Dalí's designs. The structure is thought to be the world's largest Surrealist structure. Most of his work is also displayed at the museum.

Final Years

In 1980, Dalí was forced to retire from painting due to a motor disorder that caused permanent trembling and weakness in his hands. No longer able to hold a paint brush, he even lost the ability to express himself the way he knew best. More tragedy struck in 1982, when Dalí's beloved wife and friend, Elena, died. The two events sent him into a deep depression. In 1984, Dalí was severely burned in a fire. Due to his injuries, he was confined to a wheelchair. His health continued to suffer thereafter. On January 23, 1989, Dalí died of heart failure at the age of 84.

Fast Facts

Born:	May 11, 1904
Place of Birth:	Figueres, Catalonia, Spain
Known for:	Painting, sculpture, photography, film, writing
Movement:	Cubism, Dada, Surrealism
Famous works:	The Elephants, The Persistence of Memory

Vincent Willem van Gogh

Self Portrait

Vincent van Gogh was born Vincent Willem van Gogh on March 30, 1853, in Groot-Zundert, Netherlands. His father, Theodorus van Gogh, was an austere country minister, and his mother, Anna Cornelia Carbentus, was a moody artist whose love for nature, drawing and watercolours was aptly imbibed by her son. From a young age, Van Gogh was melancholy.

When he was 15, Van Gogh's family was struggling financially, and he was forced to leave school and go to work. He secured a job at his uncle's art dealership, Goupil & Cie., a firm of art dealers in The Hague.

In June of 1873, Van Gogh was transferred to the Groupil Gallery in London. There, he fell in love with English culture. He visited art galleries in his spare time, and closely followed the writings of Charles Dickens and George Eliot. He also fell in love with his landlady's daughter, Eugenie Loyer. When she rejected his marriage proposal, Van Gogh suffered such a breakdown that he decided to devote his life to God.

Van Gogh soon started teaching in a Methodist boys' school, and preaching to the congregation. Later, hoping to become a minister, he prepared to take the entrance exam to the School of Theology in Amsterdam but later refused to take the exam.

In the winter of 1878, Van Gogh volunteered to move to an impoverished coal mine in the south of Belgium, a place where preachers were usually sent as punishment. He preached and ministered to the sick, and also drew pictures of the miners and their families, who called him "Christ of the Coal Mines." The evangelical committees were not as pleased with Van Gogh as they disagreed with Van Gogh's lifestyle. They refused to renew Van Gogh's contract, forcing him to find another occupation.

In the fall of 1880, Van Gogh decided to move to Brussels and become an artist. Though he had no formal training in art, his younger brother Theo, who worked as an art dealer, offered to support him financially. He began taking lessons on his own, studying books on art.

Van Gogh had a catastrophic love life. He was attracted to women in trouble, thinking he could help them. In 1882, Van Gogh travelled to Drenthe, a somewhat desolate district in the Netherlands. For the next six weeks, he lived a nomadic life, moving throughout the region while drawing and painting the landscape.

As an Artist

Van Gogh's art helped him stay emotionally balanced. In 1885, he began working on what is considered to be his first masterpiece, *Potato Eaters*. His brother, Theo, by this time living in Paris, believed the painting would not be well-received in the French capital, where Impressionism (use of a new scientific

Wheatfield under Thunderclouds

The Sower

research into the physics of colour to achieve a more exact representation of colour and tone) had become the trend. Nevertheless, Van Gogh decided to move to Paris, and showed up at Theo's house uninvited.

In Paris, Van Gogh first saw impressionist art, and he was inspired by the colour and light. He began studying with Henri de Toulouse-Lautrec, Pissarro and others. Van Gogh was also heavily influenced by Japanese art and began studying eastern philosophy to enhance his art and life. In February 1888, he boarded a train to the south of France. He moved into the "little yellow house" and spent his money on paint rather than food. He lived on coffee, bread and absinthe (an alcoholic drink), but soon found himself feeling sick and strange. Before long, it became apparent that in addition to suffering from physical illness, his psychological health was also declining.

Theo was worried, and offered Paul Gauguin money to go watch over Van Gogh in Arles. But Gauguin walked out after a month for he and Van Gogh constantly argued. Later, when Theo came to see his brother, the artist was very weak and had terrible seizures. After a brief stay in the hospital, Van Gogh came out alone and depressed. For hope, he turned to painting and nature, but could not find peace.

Soon, he moved to the Saint-Paul-de-Mausole asylum in Saint-Rémy-de-

Provence. On May 8, 1889, he began painting in the hospital gardens. In November 1889, he was invited to exhibit his paintings in Brussels. He sent six paintings, including *Irises* and *Starry Night*.

Death and Legacy

In early 1890, Van Gogh moved to Auvers and rented a room. In May 1890, Theo and his family visited Van Gogh, and Theo spoke to his brother about the need to be stricter with Van Gogh's finances. Van Gogh became distraught about his future, thinking that Theo meant he was no longer interested in selling his art. Two months later, Van Gogh shot himself in the chest though he survived. During his stay in the hospital, his brother was called and finally, Van Gogh asked his brother to take him home. About a month later, Van Gogh died in the arms of his brother. He was only 37 years of age.

It was only after his death that his paintings were collected and exhibited. In no time, his art had become well known. Today, Vincent Van Gogh is considered the greatest Dutch painter after Rembrandt. He completed more than 2,100 works, consisting of 860 oil paintings and more than 1,300 watercolours, drawings and sketches. Several of his paintings rank among the most expensive in the world. About 100 years later after his death, more of his artwork was discovered.

Vase with Fifteen Sunflowers

Fast Facts

Born:	March 30, 1853
Place of Birth:	Zundert, Netherlands
Known for:	Painting
Movement:	Post-Impressionism
Famous works:	The Sower, Sunflowers

Hall of Fame

Frida Kahlo
Painter

Gian Lorenzo Bernini
Sculptor

Henri Rousseau
Painter

Leonardo da Vinci
Painter, Inventor

Oscar Claude Monet
Painter

Michelangelo Buonarroti
Sculptor

Pablo Picasso
Painter, Printmaker

M.F. Husain
Painter

Rembrandt Harmenszoon van Rijn
Painter

Raphael Sanzio
Painter, Architect

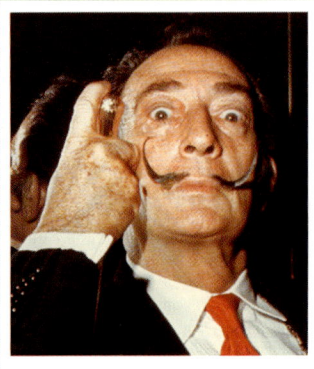
Salvador Dali
Painter, Photographer

Vincent Willem van Gogh
Painter